# Worms Are Gross!

Leigh Rockwood

**PowerKiDS**
press

New York

Published in 2011 by The Rosen Publishing Group, Inc.
29 East 21st Street, New York, NY 10010

First Edition

Editor: Maggie Murphy
Book Design: Ashley Burrell
Photo Researcher: Jessica Gerweck

Photo Credits: Cover © www.iStockphoto.com/Mikhail Kokhanchikov; p. 4 © www.iStockphoto.com/Nina Shannon; pp. 5, 12 © www.iStockphoto.com/Viorika Prikhodko; p. 6 Steve GSchmeissner/SPL/Getty Images; pp. 7, 9, 10, 13 (bottom right), 14–15, 17, 18, 20, 22 Shutterstock.com; p. 8 Kathie Atkinson/Getty Images; p. 11 © www.iStockphoto.com/Alasdair Thomson; p. 13 (top) © Rita van den Broek/age fotostock; p. 13 (bottom left) Wikipedia Commons; p. 16 DEA/Christian Ricci/Getty Images; p. 19 © www.iStockphoto.com/Suzanne Carter-Jackson; p. 21 © www.iStockphoto.com/Rainbowphoto.

Library of Congress Cataloging-in-Publication Data

Rockwood, Leigh.
  Worms are gross! / Leigh Rockwood. — 1st ed.
      p. cm. — (Creepy crawlies)
  Includes index.
  ISBN 978-1-4488-0700-0 (library binding) — ISBN 978-1-4488-1361-2 (pbk.) —
ISBN 978-1-4488-1362-9 (6-pack)
  1. Worms—Juvenile literature. I. Title.
  QL386.6.C53 2011
  592'.3—dc22

                                        2010006505

Manufactured in the United States of America

CPSIA Compliance Information: Batch #WS10PK: For Further Information contact Rosen Publishing, New York, New York at 1-800-237-9932

# Contents

If you have seen a worm wiggling on the sidewalk after a rainstorm, it was likely an earthworm! Earthworms may look like soft, slimy tubes, but they are an important link in the **food chain**. They keep the soil healthy so that plants can grow. Earthworms are also food for other animals. Did you know that if a part of an earthworm gets cut off, the lost part can sometimes grow back? This is called **regeneration**.

Earthworms feel slimy and wet. Some people think they are too gross to touch!

▶

Did you know that in 1 acre (.4 ha) of land, you might find more than one million earthworms in the ground?

There are many gross animals called worms, but not all of these worms are closely related to earthworms. Many of these other worms are parasites, or animals that live in, on, or with another living thing. However, earthworms live on their own.

# Segmented Worms

Earthworms belong to a group of animals called annelids. Annelids are known as **segmented** worms. Look closely at an earthworm's body, and you will see rings going around its tubelike body. Each of these rings is a segment. An earthworm's body has a **nervous system**, a **digestive system**, and a **circulatory system**,

This is a close-up photograph of an earthworm's body. Here you can see its segments.

which pumps blood. These body systems are found in people, too, but they are much more complex in people than in earthworms.

How does an earthworm move? Each segment has two pairs of hairlike parts called setae. The setae hold on to the ground as the worm uses its muscles to make a wavelike movement that goes from the back of its body forward.

7

There are more than 4,000 **species** of earthworms in the world. Scientists divide these species into three groups, based on where in the soil the species lives.

**Epigeic** worms, such as the red wiggler, live among plant litter, or dead plant matter, in shallow, loose soil. This is the kind of worm

Unlike endogeic and anecic earthworms, epigeic earthworms live near or on the surface of the ground.

This photo shows an earthworm pulling a leaf down into its vertical burrow.

often found in backyards. **Endogeic** worms build horizontal, branching burrows. They do not often come up to the surface. **Anecic** worms, such as night crawlers, build deep vertical burrows and come up to the surface to feed. Anecic worms coat their burrows with **mucus**. This slimy stuff helps keep the burrow from falling in.

Earthworms live all over the world. Their **habitats** range from just above ground to many feet (m) under ground, depending on which species of worm it is. Epigeic worms live in wet, shallow soil and among rotting plant matter on the ground. Endogeic and anecic worms live in burrows that they dig in the ground. Anecic worms dig the deepest burrows. They often dig about 6 feet (2 m) under ground.

Here, an earthworm moves among wet fallen tree leaves.

This earthworm is burrowing in soil. It can breathe underground as long as the soil is not too wet.

Earthworms' bodies dry out quickly when they are away from their wet homes. When there is a heavy rain, however, the soil gets too wet for worms. They breathe air, and the wet soil can drown worms. This forces them to leave their burrows to keep from drowning.

# Life Cycle

**1**

Baby earthworms hatch from cocoons. When they hatch, they are only .5 to 1 inch (1–2.5 cm) long. These worms will reach full size at about one year old, but they can have babies in only six weeks.

**2**

An earthworm has both male and female parts. That means that an earthworm can **mate** with any other worm of the same species. When they mate, each worm helps the other worm **fertilize** the eggs in its body.

The cocoons an earthworm makes are much smaller than a grain of rice! They are yellow in color. The cocoons keep baby worms safe. Sometimes soil is too dry for the baby worms. When this happens, the cocoon can remain dormant, or alive but not active, for years until it is safe for the babies to hatch.

During mating, a cocoon forms on a wide segment, called the clitellum, on each worm's body. The worms then back out of these cocoons and place them in the soil. The cocoons will hatch two to three weeks later.

**3**

# Fact Sheet: GROSS!

**1** Worms are cold-blooded animals, as are many reptiles, amphibians, and fish.

**2** Earthworms do not have arms or legs, but they do have five tiny hearts!

**3** Even though they do not have eyes, worms can sense light. However, if they spend too much time in direct light, they can become paralyzed. This means they cannot move!

**4** Most earthworms found in the United States are between 6 and 11 inches (15–28 cm) long. In Australia and South America, there are giant earthworms that can grow to a length of 11 feet (3 m)!

It is possible to hear giant earthworms wiggling underground. Their movement makes a gurgling sound.

**5**

Scientists think that earthworms have lived on Earth for over 500 million years.

**6**

Anecic worms build little mounds of dirt and pebbles near the entrances of their burrows. This helps them find their burrows when they are done feeding aboveground.

**7**

Some earthworms have a bad-tasting mucus that they let out when they are trying to get away from another animal.

**8**

# Good for the Soil

The earthworm eats rotting plant litter and soil as it moves through the dirt. If a worm cannot fit a bit of food into its mouth, it will first make it wet and soft, then suck it into its mouth. Anything that the worm does not use to live leaves as waste through the other end of its body.

The waste that earthworms make, shown here, is called cast.

Here, a gardener is happy to find earthworms in his garden. The worms mix up the soil so plants can grow there.

The digging, eating, and getting rid of waste that earthworms do is good for the soil. The worm's digging keeps the soil loose so that air and water can easily move through it. Breaking down plant waste mixes the soil and keeps it full of **nutrients**. This makes the soil good for growing plants.

# Red Wigglers

Red wigglers are a kind of epigeic earthworm. They get their name from their dark, brownish red color. Red wigglers are big eaters for their size. They eat at least half their body weight in food every day!

Red wigglers are often used in fishing as bait. People also use red wigglers to break down

This red wiggler is being put on to a fishhook to be used as bait.

Red wigglers are good composting worms because they live in big groups and do not dig deep burrows.

garbage into **compost** for their gardens. These worms wiggle their way through loose, shallow soil to eat dirt, rotting plants and food, and even animal waste. That sounds like a gross dinner to you, but red wigglers love it! The worms mix up the soil and compost and keep them full of nutrients for growing plants.

# Food and Defenses

Earthworms are at the bottom of many food chains. That means they are small animals that are eaten by bigger animals. These bigger animals are, in turn, eaten by bigger or stronger animals. Birds, snakes, frogs, skunks, and bugs are among the animals that eat earthworms.

This blackbird caught a wiggly, dirt-covered earthworm for lunch!

Here, a frog snacks on an unlucky earthworm.

Earthworms can feel movement on the ground. If they feel an animal coming, they try to get as far down into the soil as they can. If an animal still catches an earthworm by its tail, the worm uses its setae to hold on to its burrow's walls. If part of the worm breaks off in this tug-of-war, the worm can regenerate some of its lost segments!

# Slimy, Wiggly, Cool

Worms are gross, but it is fun to know how they make their grossness work for them. Mucus is more than just slimy stuff! It keeps worms from drying out and helps hold their burrows together. The next time you see earthworms, you will know that they

Wiggling may look creepy, but those waves of movement let worms move and dig without having feet.

have an important place in the food chain. Worms add nutrients to the soil that grows our fruits and vegetables. Worms feed animals that people eat, such as chickens. Earthworms are slimy and wiggly, but they are an important part of life on Earth!

# Glossary

**anecic** (uh-NEE-sik) Living in deep burrows but feeding near the surface.

**circulatory system** (SER-kyuh-luh-tor-ee SIS-tem) The path by which blood travels through the body.

**compost** (KOM-pohst) A mixture of broken-down matter that makes soil richer.

**digestive system** (dy-JES-tiv SIS-tem) The body parts that help turn food into the power a body needs.

**endogeic** (en-doh-JEE-ik) Always making burrows under ground.

**epigeic** (eh-pih-JEE-ik) Living on or near the surface of the ground.

**fertilize** (FUR-tuh-lyz) To put male cells inside an egg to make babies.

**food chain** (FOOD CHAYN) A group of living things that are one another's food.

**habitats** (HA-buh-tats) The kinds of land where animals or plants naturally live.

**mate** (MAYT) To come together to make babies.

**mucus** (MYOO-kus) Thick, slimy matter produced by the bodies of many animals.

**nervous system** (NER-vus SIS-tum) The system of nerves in people or animals.

**nutrients** (NOO-tree-unts) Food that a living thing needs to live and grow.

**regeneration** (rih-jeh-nuh-RAY-shun) Growing or producing something again.

**segmented** (SEG-men-ted) Having many smaller pieces.

**species** (SPEE-sheez) One kind of living thing. All people are one species.

# Index

# Web Sites

Due to the changing nature of Internet links, PowerKids Press has developed an online list of Web sites related to the subject of this book. This site is updated regularly. Please use this link to access the list: www.powerkidslinks.com/creep/worm/